W9-AVC-517

DISCARDED

DISCARDED

What Has Small Arms and **Jagged Teeth**?

WRITTEN BY **Robert Kanner**

ILLUSTRATED BY **Russ Daff**

dingles & company New Jersey

IN MEMORY OF MY FATHER, WHO ALLOWED ME TO FIND MY OWN VOICE

© 2008 dingles & company

ALL RIGHTS RESERVED
No part of this book may be reproduced in any form without written
permission from the publishers, except by a reviewer who may quote
brief passages in a review to be printed in a newspaper or magazine.

First Printing

Published by dingles&company
P.O. Box 508
Sea Girt, New Jersey 08750

LIBRARY OF CONGRESS
CATALOG CARD NUMBER
2007904353

ISBN
978-1-59646-836-8

Printed in the United States
of America

The Uncover & Discover series is
based on the original concept
of Judy Mazzeo Zocchi.

ART DIRECTION & DESIGN
Rizco Design

EDITORIAL CONSULTANT
Andrea Curley

PROJECT MANAGER
Lisa Aldorasi

EDUCATIONAL CONSULTANTS
Melissa Oster and Margaret Bergin

CREATIVE DIRECTOR
Barbie Lambert

PRE-PRESS
Pixel Graphics

WEBSITE
www.dingles.com

E-MAIL
info@dingles.com

J567.9
KAN

The Uncover & Discover series encourages children to inquire, investigate, and use their imagination in an interactive and entertaining manner. This series helps to sharpen their powers of observation, improve reading and writing skills, and apply knowledge across the curriculum.

Uncover each one and see you can when you're

clue one by what dinosaur discover done!

My large **eyes** sit at the front of my head, facing forward. This helps me spot my prey more easily.

WHERE IS THE **EYE**?

I have a narrow **snout**
and a sharp sense of smell.
This helps me find the
animals I eat.

LOOK FOR THE **SNOUT**.

My big, powerful **jaws** open
3 feet wide. I can chomp
hundreds of pounds of meat
and bones in one bite!

FIND THE **JAWS**.

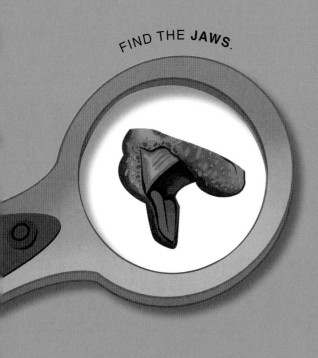

I use my 11-inch-long, razor-sharp front **teeth** to grasp my prey. Shorter, jagged back teeth allow me to rip through thick skin.

DO YOU SEE THE **TEETH?**

My short and muscular **neck** helps support my 5-foot-long head.

WHERE IS THE **NECK?**

My bony, scaly **skin**
looks as if it has
pebbles all over it.

LOOK FOR THE **SKIN**.

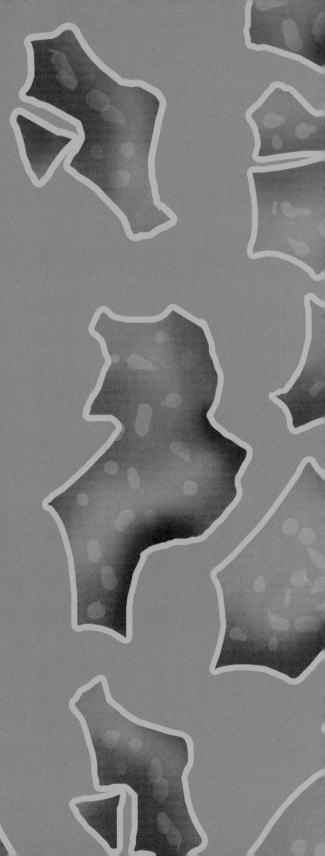

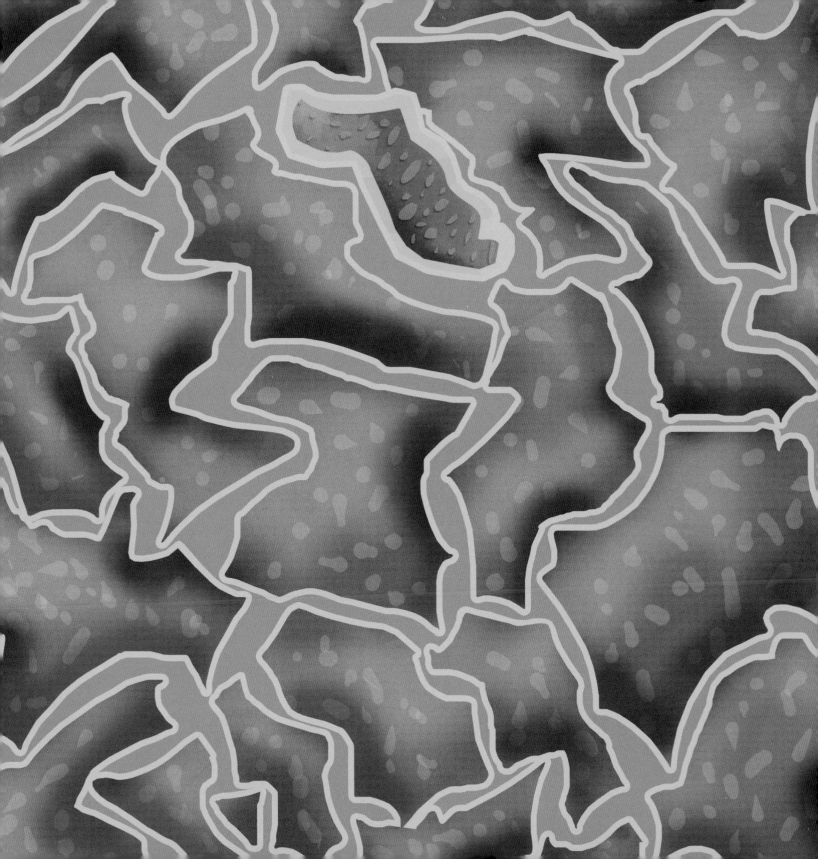

I use my short, muscular **arms**
to push my heavy body up
from a lying-down position.

FIND THE **ARM**.

My tiny arms have two fingers with **claws** at the end of each of them. I use these claws to hold onto my prey while I'm eating it.

DO YOU SEE THE **CLAWS**?

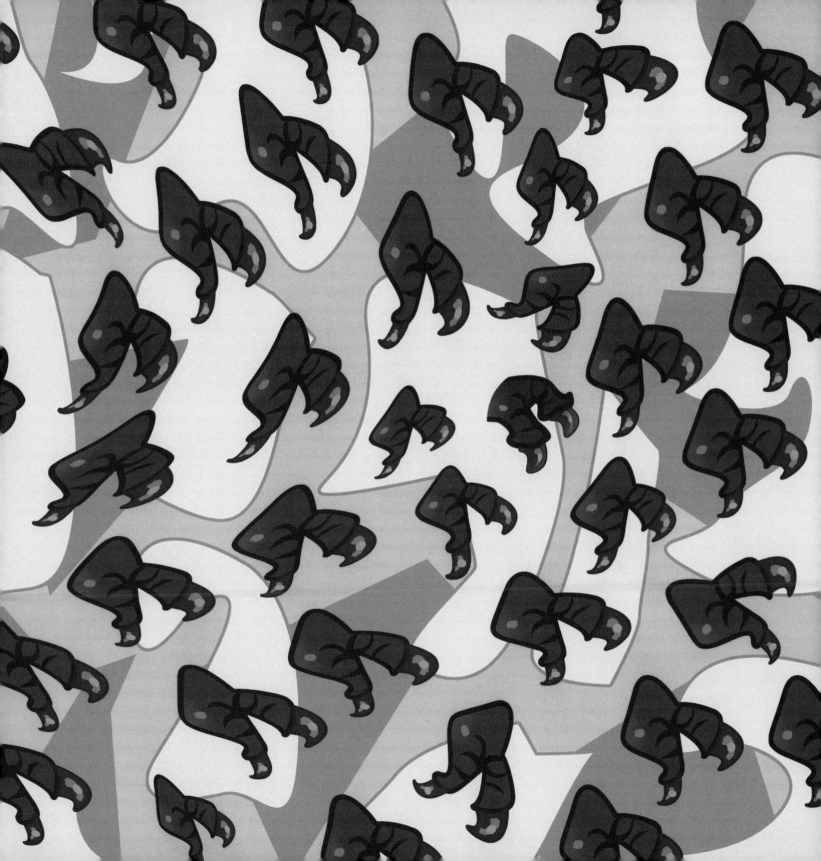

Large, powerful **legs** allow me to walk long distances and to run up to 15 miles per hour.

WHERE IS THE **LEG?**

My narrow **feet** point down.
This makes me walk or run
on my toes.

LOOK FOR THE **FOOT**.

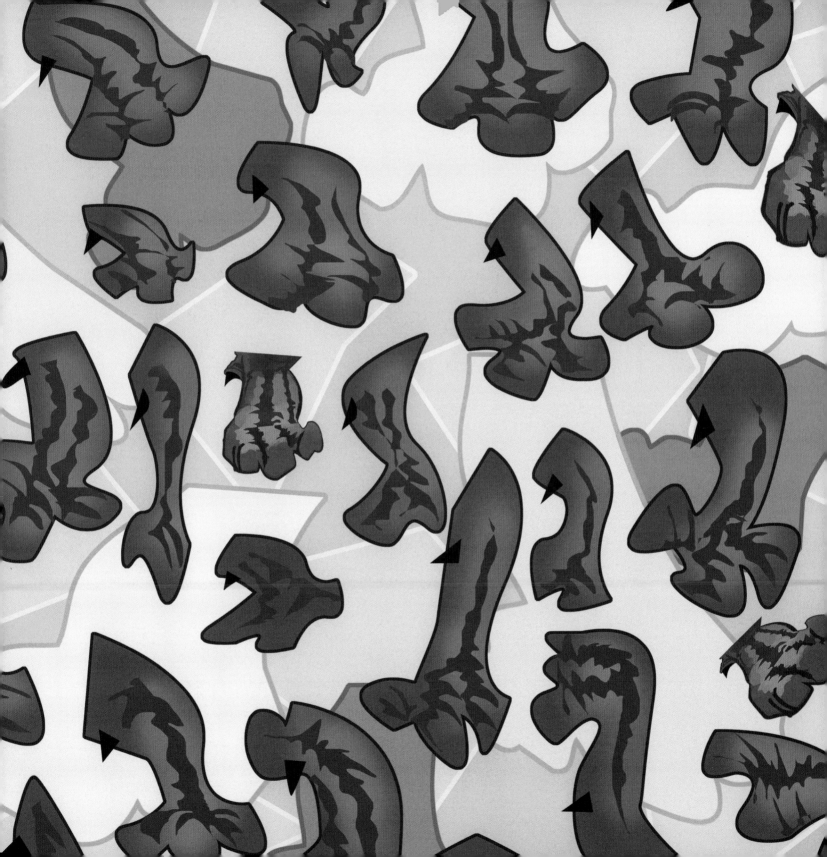

Each of my feet has three clawed **toes** in the front and one toe in the back.

FIND THE **TOES**.

A stiff, pointed **tail** helps me balance myself so I can make quick turns when I run.

DO YOU SEE THE **TAIL**?

You have uncovered the clues. **Have you guessed what I am?**

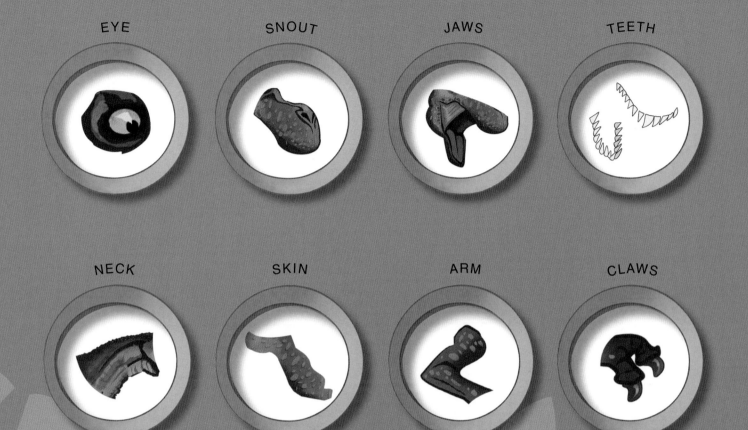

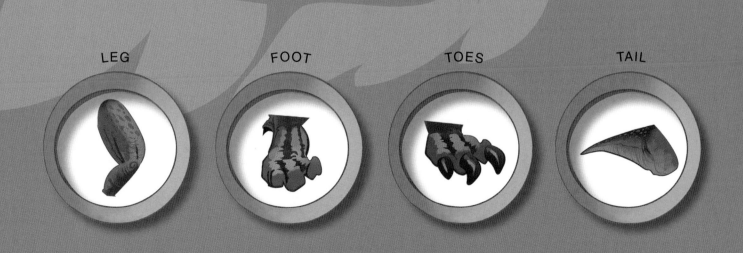

EYE

SNOUT

JAWS

TEETH

NECK

SKIN

ARM

CLAWS

LEG

FOOT

TOES

TAIL

If not, here are more clues.

1. I am a prehistoric reptile that lives on the land.

2. I am one of the largest of a group of dinosaurs that walk on two legs. Like the others in my group, I have birdlike claws; sharp, slicing teeth; a short neck; a stiff tail; and large, powerful legs.

3. My huge head is 5 feet long!

4. I am about 40 feet long (about the length of a commuter bus) and about 15 feet tall.

5. I weigh around 12,000 pounds (about the same as an elephant).

6. I run about 15 miles per hour (the average human runs about 6-8 mph).

7. I was hatched from an egg.

8. I live in a region that is now western North America.

9. I am a carnivore, which means I am a meat eater.

Now add

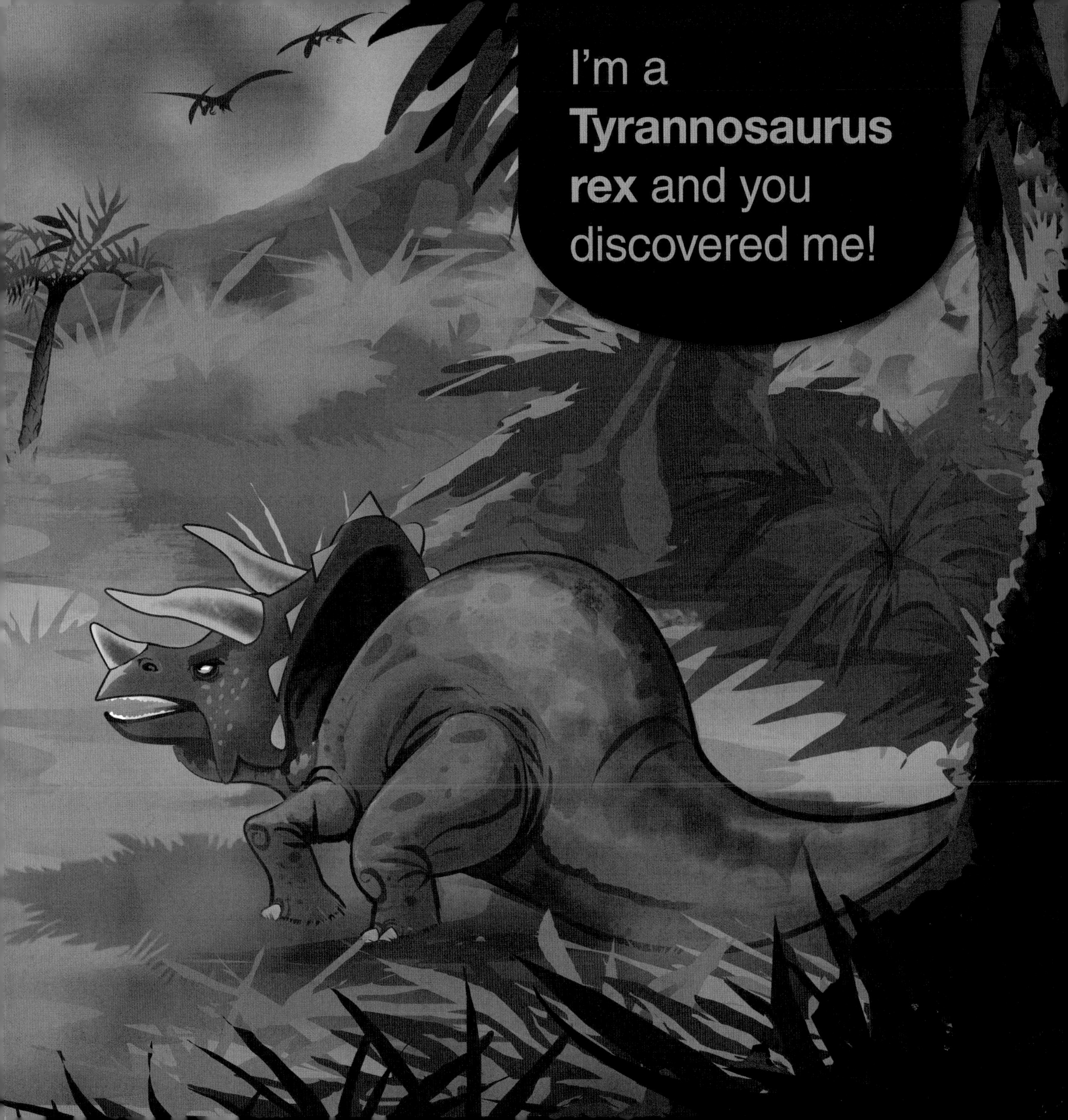
I'm a **Tyrannosaurus rex** and you discovered me!

Do you want to know more about me? Here are some *Tyrannosaurus rex* fun facts.

1. *Tyrannosaurus rex* (tuh-ran-uh-SAWR-us rex) means "tyrant lizard king." This name indicates that scientists think this was one of the most ferocious dinosaurs that ever lived.

2. *Tyrannosaurus rex* lived during the late Cretaceous period, about 85 to 65 million years ago, a time when there were severe climate changes, earthquakes, and volcanic eruptions.

3. *Tyrannosaurus rex* is one of the largest known meat eaters. It ate large dinosaurs such as *Triceratops*.

4. *Tyrannosaurus rex* had long, jagged teeth. When they got old and worn, new ones grew in to replace them.

5. Scientists think that *Tyrannosaurus rex* had an excellent sense of smell–a large area of its brain seemed to have been used to figure out what different smells were.

6. The largest *Tyrannosaurus rex* skeleton fossil ever discovered was found in 1990 in South Dakota. The tyrannosaur was named Sue after Sue Hendrickson, the scientist who discovered the fossil skeleton.

7. *Tyrannosaurus rex* and all other dinosaurs disappeared about 65 million years ago. It is widely believed that a giant asteroid or comet hit Earth and caused major climactic changes to which the dinosaurs couldn't adapt.

8. The first *Tyrannosaurus rex* fossil was found by Barnum Brown, a paleontologist (a scientist who learns about prehistoric life-forms by studying fossils), in 1902. He discovered it in Hell Creek, Montana. It was named by paleontologist Henry Osborn in 1905.

Who, What, Where, When, Why, and How

USE THE QUESTIONS who, what, where, when, why, and how to help the child apply knowledge and process the information in the book. Encourage him or her to investigate, inquire, and imagine.

In the Book...

DO YOU KNOW WHO found the largest *Tyrannosaurus rex* skeleton fossil in 1990?

DO YOU KNOW WHAT the featured dinosaur in the book is?

DO YOU KNOW WHERE the first *Tyrannosaurus rex* fossil was found?

DO YOU KNOW WHEN *Tyrannosaurus rex* lived?

DO YOU KNOW WHY scientists think *Tyrannosaurus rex* had an excellent sense of smell?

DO YOU KNOW HOW fast *Tyrannosaurus rex* could run?

In Your Life...

Tyrannosaurus rex was a prehistoric reptile that lived on land. What modern-day reptiles live on land?

CROSS-CURRICULAR EXTENSIONS

Math

Tyrannosaurus rex weighed about 12,000 pounds. How may tons would *Tyrannosaurus rex* weigh (1 ton equals 2,000 pounds)?

Science

Tyrannosaurus rex lived during the Cretaceous period, about 85 to 65 million years ago. Do some investigating to find out what period we live in today.

Social Studies

The first *Tyrannosaurus rex* fossil was found in the state of Montana. What states border Montana?

Fun Activity

You have uncovered the clues and discovered *Tyrannosaurus rex*.

ASSIGNMENT
Write a riddle about *Tyrannosaurus rex*.

USE THE ANSWERS TO THE QUESTIONS BELOW TO CREATE YOUR RIDDLE
Who was afraid of *Tyrannosaurus rex*?
What did *Tyrannosaurus rex* look like?
Where did *Tyrannosaurus rex* live?
When did *Tyrannosaurus rex* live?
Why won't you see *Tyrannosaurus rex* roaming the earth now?
How much did *Tyrannosaurus rex* weigh?

WRITE
Enjoy the writing process while you take what you have imagined and create your riddle.

UNCOVER
&DISCOVER

Author

Robert Kanner is part of the writing team for the Uncover
& Discover series as well as the Global Adventures and
Holiday Happenings series. An extensive career in the film
and television business includes work as a film acquisition
executive at the Walt Disney Company, a story editor for
a children's television series, and an independent family-
film producer. He holds a bachelor's degree in psychology
from the University of Buffalo and lives in the Hollywood
Hills, California, with Tom and Miss Murphy May.

Illustrator

Since graduating from Falmouth School of Art in 1993,
Russ Daff has enjoyed a varied career. For eight years
he worked on numerous projects in the computer games
industry, producing titles for Sony PlayStation and PC
formats. While designing a wide range of characters
and environments for these games, he developed a
strong sense of visual impact that he later utilized in his
illustration and comic work. Russ now concentrates on
his illustration and cartooning full-time. When he is not
working, he enjoys painting, writing cartoon stories, and
playing bass guitar. He lives in Cambridge, England.